The Evolution of Music by Jerry Ingeman

War Surrounds Us

Michael Dickel

2015

Poetry

War Surrounds Us ©2015 Michael Dickel. No part of this book may be reproduced in any manner whatsoever, including electronic or online formats, without written permission except for brief quotations embedded in critical articles and reviews.

Cover art: *The Evolution of Music* ©2015 Jerry Ingeman *Repeated on the frontispiece and details used on section heading pages.*

is a rose press publishes poetry, poetics, experimental writing, cross-genre and other work. We are a cooperative editorial board of writers in the virtual world. Submissions are by invitation only at this time. Check our website for updates and changes in this policy.

Website: isarosepress.WordPress.com

Dickel, Michael (b. 1955)
    War Surrounds Us

      is a rose press
      1. Poetry. 2. Peace Poetry 3. Israel. 4. Middle East.

      I. Title: War Surrounds Us.

ISBN   978-0-9896245-2-7

War Surrounds Us

Prologue—Breaking News

Another term for counterpoint—"...disphony...[stands] for music in which the different parts have different pitches and are relatively independent rhythmically." Malm, W. P. (1972) On the Meaning and Invention of the Term "Disphony." Ethnomusicology. 16:2 (May). pp. 247–249.

Breaking News

In a country where I no longer live
the Fourth of July arrived today amid
parades and fireworks
                    even while
citizens divided, not united, debate
uncivilly about guns, birth control,
rights and economics for the thrill
of it all.

            The feudal corporate rulers
unduly control the terms and conditions
of the discourse, determine by their rule
who may speak and who will listen.
Not you or me.

                I turn to news updates
here in my new home. Found-discord a
modern composition in disphony—

"Clashes break out on the Temple Mount"
shortly after 1 P.M.; at nearly 3 P.M.

"Hateful inscription against Arabs
spray scrawled in Ashdod"
                        ten minutes
later, "Vandals spray paint swastikas,
'Death to Jews' in Rahat"
                        then "Funeral
procession of Palestinian teen
Muhammad Abu Khdeir begins"
                        by four

"Code red siren blares in Eshkol;
rocket fired at IDF forces hits open area"

"35 lightly wounded in east Jerusalem clashes"

by six "Gaza rocket strikes Kibbutz in south
damaging buildings"
                         at seven "13 police officers
wounded in East Jerusalem riots"

                         inevitably
around 8:30 "IAF launches attacks
on terror targets in Gaza"
                         and shortly after
"Civilians in south warned to stay
within 15 second of bomb shelters"

                         and
an hour later, "Gaza rocket lands in open area."

And who may speak? Who will listen?

Not you or me. We already have our opinions.
certified, stamped, approved and strongly held.

Fires

Tires burn as souls turn
from compassion to hurt,
then twist to anger,
as both sides shout
calls for vengeance.

Stones fly from slingshots,
hardened from hearts
torn apart by pain.
Murdered teens
on both sides,

the killers dark
purveyors of death
lighting dry tinder
drenched in gasoline—

like the body of the boy
burned while still alive,

like three shot and left
to rot under rocks
in a dry field.

The eight parents'
tears won't teach the furrows
to grow food—
               the only
fruit here a bitter violence
on all sides, police beatings,
riots, children hurt by objects
thrown through car windows
while riding toward summer
vacation.

       Where do we go
from here? What will we see
that would help us to turn
to the other in weeping?
Why don't our tears
quench these fires?

Crossing

Crossing languages might be easier
than crossing borders, even where
people share the same tongue—
those political lines we draw,
the religious barriers we raise,
the constructions of Otherness
and Us-ness—
           all the legacy
of Babel, our raised pride—a tower
built from ideologies and beliefs, cold
stones shaped by history, geology—
that would challenge the mystery
of tree buds
           which start to swell,
once the days begin slowly,
oh so slowly, to grow even
in the midst of frigid winter.

Again

The world has gone mad. Again.
And again voices incite—then hoarse leaders
pretend to have been polite. They did not shout
fear and hatred to explosive tension, to a thin-
wire stretched, first sounding a note then cracking,
snapping in two, each piece twisted. The world goes
mad. Again. The leaders call for calm, like arsonists
who work in the fire department. The fires burn
in the streets at night. The checkpoints flow
with blood and tears. And most of us just want
to go to work, have coffee with friends, teach
our children something other than this craziness
in a world gone mad. Again. And most of us want
to turn away and not see the burning, the smoke,
the arsonists lining up toy soldiers at borders
ready to pounce, to attack, to burn. Again.

War Surrounds Us

Life as you knew it

The booms sound serious—
not Bastille Day fireworks,
nor Fourth of July blasts,
but something akin to these—
like you're in town that night
and decided to stay home
anyway, so you hear the thuds
echoing across the lake
along some valley. Yet there
is no lake here, although
plenty of valleys. And you're
outside, sitting in your car
in a parking lot thinking
about heading home
when you hear the booms.
They sound serious,
those rockets exploding
in air hit by contrarian
missiles that took them
down somewhere else.
You know where the
Code Red sounded,
near the beach you like,
and it's not very near,
but apparently near enough
as the echoes speak to you
and tell you that this is not
what you planned and this
is not what they planned
which seems to be, what
they planned is to kill you,
but not really you, just
someone like you or anyone
really who happened

to answer the call of
the booms knocking at
that last door just before
they explode into your life
or possibly, that is, the end
of your life as you knew it.
And you hear in the echoes
how contrarian missiles explode
and end their lives, too,
known and unknown.

The bomb shelter

Yesterday, I went along on the pre-school
field trip to the fire station. We sprayed
water from a firehose and the wind
blew back a cooling mist from the hot
day. Moshe loved watching the hose
stream its white plume out into the air
like fire behind a rocket, perhaps.

You see, last night the sirens blew,
sweat dripped down as I carried
sleeping Moshe to the bomb shelter
where he woke, his body hot with fever.
Friends we never saw in pajamas before,
neighbors holding children as we did,
older children chattering with each other—

all gathered into this armored room,
all looking around at each other all
a bit lost, a bit amused, a lot worried.

And somewhere nearby white
plumes streamed behind rockets.
We heard two thudding booms
like distant construction or fireworks,
and it was over. No cool mist
blew back on us, no relief from the heat.

The roses

A humanitarian ceasefire brought quiet
for a couple of hours, at least, although
a few rockets just flew out of Gaza.
These things happen—unfortunately.
In a few hours the short ceasefire
retires but what happens next depends
on people in separate rooms of a Cairo
hotel and mediators running between.

Like most days, my son went to preschool.
My daughter plays in her daycare. My wife
has gone to work. Papers wait for me
to read them and students wait to hear
their grades. Clouds watch indifferently.
Only my mind seems restless,
impatient, listening for the cracks,
the siren call, the singing voice
that will seduce me with rage, until
I crash against an ideological cliff.

A large half-moon shone in the morning's
bright-cerulean sky. Yellow roses passed
their prime along the walk, but the crimson
bud—no, perhaps more a claret color—
tightly wraps its future, which is ready to burst
out and declare a moment's respite
like a five-hour ceasefire, or like a truce
without resolution of all the injustices
on both sides, without grief for all the dead
on both sides, without a care in the world
except to bloom beautifully under a
clear sky and a setting moon.

Perhaps this is a good thing, I don't know.
Who am I to judge a flower? Perhaps
I should go to the beach and watch waves
to learn about the futility of words and ideas.
Maybe it would be better to rest, take a nap,
dream. Instead, I write this poem, this fantasy
of connecting to you, my enemy, my lover across
the border, and finding a common ground
where we might plant our gardens together.
Will you hear the boom of this poem
the next time a jet drops a bomb near you?
And your poetry, will I recognize it as it
flies toward me and explodes? Will you
write it gently, so that I might catch it?

Massacre

It could be a massacre of language,
its definition though is indiscriminate
deliberate brutal killing of (many)
people. It's just after Bastille Day
and back then we know, there
were real massacres. Today
nearly two-hundred have died
so far, and yes, some were children.
Many people, then. And each
life worthy of grief, each child
doubly so. I'm American, I'm used
to others killing in my name,
it comes with the paperwork.

Yet this is more intimate,
closer, rockets aimed at me,
too, even if ineffectively.
Over one-thousand six-hundred
the number of air strikes
in Gaza, thunderous rage
poured out in retaliation
answered by more rockets
in retaliation, the self-devouring
snake that unites us.

Such an incompetent
massacre, the killing
so efficient that the
accountants can easily
do the math, tally
the price, and move on.

Each dead child's
parents—torn apart
and left to bleed slowly
to death, while breathing
and walking and working—
counted.

        And the retaliation
continues, reptilian and cold,
retaliation the perpetrator
of all massacres.

Mosquitos

i

That some of those labelled as enemies
have crossed the lines to offer condolences
at the mourning tents; that the mourning
families spoke to each other as parents
and cried on each others' shoulders;
that we cried for the children who died
on both sides of the divide; that the
war began anyway; that hope must
still remain with those who cross
borders, ignore false lines and divisions;
that children should be allowed to live;
that we must cry for all children who die;

for all of this, dear owl mothers
whose children have been murdered,
do not call the sun to the dawn.
Let us suffer the night of losses.

ii

As the darkness settles the dust,
come, hear the witnesses
tell the lion what they know—
from the end to the beginning.

Let us find the mosquito who started
it all with his lies and rumors
in the African tale.

iii

First, we learn that the monkey
killed your child. The monkey
ran, alarmed by the crow's call.
The crow called out warning
when the rabbit ran, afraid.
The rabbit was scared by
the python, who crept into
its hole. The python feared
that the lizard had plotted
against it. The lizard simply
hadn't heard a word.

iv

                      It
had blocked its ears,
in denial of mosquito
propaganda, the lies
and rumors of death,
the drawing of lines
that divide us with
verbs we cannot
put objects to, do
not know subjects
for. Do not call
the sun to the
dawn. Leave
us suffering
in the night
of losses.

The Cost of Yellow

I know there's a war going on,
but yellow flowers cover trees
in the parking lot as I pull in.
True, missiles shatter lives
while destroying buildings, but
fallen petals cover the tarmac
with a fairy-yellow glow. Yes,
sirens send us underground
while rocket's dread flares,
and these too crash
stupendously, but the
sea air waves a soft, humid
blanket spread out by
soothing breezes. So
easily I forget the price
of wind, the cost of yellow;
so hard to forget the lone
cry of a carrion crow
perched high in the tree
with sharp eyes turned
toward the horizon.

Nightmare

I recollected it when I woke,
gathering its pieces to me.
My children were all three
years old. They wrote on
paper sandwiched between
thin strips of color, construction-
paper covers. They worked
on invitations. Each child
intent on drawing the words
carefully in legal-pad yellow
crayon; each word large and
carefully printed in child's hand.
The words rose from the paper,
yellow and translucent, beautiful
as daffodil petals. They floated
up around the children as sirens
sounded everywhere—not just here,
but also there. The words were one
word repeated three times:

Weep. Weep. Weep.

Poster war

What if they gave a war and nobody came?
—the poster reads. Too late. The invitations
engraved, have gone out; the RSVPs were sent;
the guests, always arriving dressed to kill.
The caterers insist that the show must go on.
The musicians composed their anthems.
The writers polished their prose to a sharp point.
And so the party begins, the blood pours
from the punch bowls, brains and entrails
serve as unappetizing appetizers. Fires burn
in every corner and soon the smoke covers
the last bits of truth. We hear each other
only distantly, we talk hesitantly or shout
hatefully. The dance of death strikes midnight,
the skull calling the steps. Children cry;
adults tremble with fear and righteousness,
each sure of being right, each afraid of being
wrong. What if they gave a war, and nobody
came? Too late. The engraved invitations
were welcomed, gathered in, tied with ribbons.

Musical Meditations

Qanun like a zither plucking
running goats from a carousing stream,
Saz strings singing each water drop,
Oud shaking the rainbow from the mist,
Kamanjah—that other name for a violin—
surfing along the ultraviolet waves,
while a Russian *Balalaika* taps
its toes frenetically and
the *Darbuka* keeps them in time
and sometimes Bongos serve
for *Tablas*—all a whirling meditation
chorusing the heavens in hopes
that one day their peace will come
as Arab and Jew play a concert together
on a mystical mountain in the Upper Galilee.

Lessons

Ruhama told our Moshe before he
turned three, when she met him that first school day,
that she had a Moshe at home, her son.
She often reminded him of that fact.
The evening of Moshe's last day in class
we learn that Ruhama's Moshe was killed
in Gaza that day. So many have died.
And what do we tell our Moshe about
his own future, desire for lasting peace,
about life and death, so many deaths now,
and Ruhama, who no longer has her
Moshe at home, who today buried him
as thousands bury their children in so
many places: Gaza, Syria, Iraq,
Nigeria, Somalia, Yemen—
the names do not end...the teacher's lesson
not what we hoped...geography of death.

Barometric pressure dropping

Clouds pace across the sun, ice shadows
chilling ground where they block the light—
shadows—

like blood stains on a prayer shawl,
pooled blood on the floor—
dark stains—

waiting for people to drink it up,
taste fear, feed the deep anger—
ancient—

rage burning like the sun
behind the coming storm—
ruins—

what brought breath now consuming it.

As the War Continues

i

That war in the little southwest strip,
its violence drowns out all sounds—
words drain of meaning and become
white spaces against blood-red paper.
The numbers rise up, a large pile
of bodies reaching toward the sun
to ignite and burn, a pyre signaling
the beginning or end of a sacred time—

ii

the bodies pile up, reach for the sun,
hoping to burn like stars to light this dark,
dark night...
      but we all seem to have lost track,
our watches no longer ticking but
vibrating with technical accuracy
seconds and micro-seconds while
this flame of flesh, a mere candle wick,

iii

flashes out into space in search
of extraterrestrial compassion. And
Gaza's heavenward tower of bodily Babel
ieven shrinks small against so many others,
this massive world-war of death
spreading out around us while we
shout out who is to blame, who
except for ourselves, ourselves

iv
turning away into silence and denial,
pointing at someone easier than seeing
a world around us in un-holy flames
cremating the innocent along with
the bloody-handed ones. Yet,
the sunset is so beautiful below
the clouds and over the sea, the
moon so light floating in the sky
above an orange cloud on this Tu B'Av.

War Surrounds Us

i

We have been in the north for a while, in Tzfat,
on the mystical mountain across from Meron.
When we arrived, rockets still flew toward Jerusalem—
one the evening we left, another a few days later. The IDF
continued to pound Gaza, soldiers remained in embattled
streets, engineers destroyed tunnels, civilians died.

ii

Slowly, our son's discussion of rockets shifts
and he builds fewer with his blocks and Legos,
although they have not totally disappeared even though

iii

now a five-day ceasefire extension added
to a seventy-two hour one that held join with
talks in Cairo that pretend enough seriousness
to end this battle.
               The war?
                          That will continue…
                                                …it doesn't stop.

iv

These few weeks we have swum with Palestinians
in the Sea of Galilee, smiled with Arabs as our
children's ice creams melted in the summer sun.
We rode tour boats where we danced with Arabs and Jews.

v

Today we picked apples in the Golan within sight
of the Syrian border and heard the rumbling war there,
booming canon and mortar echoing across heated hills.
Our son overhears our discussion with an orchard worker—
who moved here to raise his kids outside of the city—

and our boy wants to see the booms. We tell him
they are over the hills, which satisfies him for now.
He happily rides in the trailer behind the tractor on
our way to the rows of ripe Galas and Sandras
overlooking the *Quneitra* Crossing.

vi
What will we say to him about his time to join the army?

vii
The wind blew strong from behind. And after the apples,
sitting in shade, playing with our young children,
we found three peacock feathers and a goose quill
on the ground. As we drove away, the thunder
rumbled a few rounds from the right, a few from the left.

viii
We ate lunch in a Druze village—a table full of salads,
majadra, chicken, lamb, hummus—a smiley-face
with Hebrew and Arabic for the name of the cafe.
Out front, parked next to our car, a Massey-Ferguson
tractor. It reminds me of rural Minnesota, this
tractor outside the cafe—like Hinckley, site of the
Great Fire that glowed on skylines a hundred miles
distant and melted railroad tracks—it's like being there,
sitting at the A&W with a rootbeer float and watching.

Except for the Arabic, the Hebrew…
                       the thunder of war just over the horizon.

In Tzfat this Evening

The Klezmer festival music plays on
and the fireworks blast into the sky
exactly on time at ten, brilliant and loud.
But the ceasefire broke apart before
then, hours before—and Code Red
sirens blasted in the South, in Tel Aviv,
in Jerusalem, shortly after that. Followed
by artillery shelling and air bombardment
in Gaza, that small contested strip. Still,
sitting in the courtyard we hear
music from three stages echoing
around us.

                Moshe's Lego rockets became
fishing rockets and fireworks rockets here,
but when we go back they will remember
that they are Hamas rockets. The Legos
fit together so well. He builds them like
planes, with wings, and like spaceships,
with elaborate purposes and missions.

Tonight he enjoyed the fireworks;
he wants them every night. These
first rockets an aesthetic echo of
war rockets; a rhetorical trope to
resemble tractors where spears
fly into the sky at night and clatter
loudly in our conscious minds—enter
our sleep and crack open our fears.

And I imagine Gazan children who
will find fear in fireworks, only fear—
reminders of destruction instead
of wonders of color and light.

ii
Like last night, when I dreamed that
a mortar shell came over the Quneitra
Crossing while we picked apples, and
tore you apart. I took the children
away from the burning orchards
and woke to a small miracle—
you breathing next to me,
our children sleeping calmly.

iii
Let Lego rockets take the weapons
into space and carry them into the sun.

Let us watch the lovely fireworks
as they burst open approaching

our star, explode amid the melted
plastic of a child's imagination

run up against the realities of
fire, heat, fusion—physics

teaching adults that entropy wins.
Even the Klezmer music must stop.

But the wonder and the fear of children
continue to grow—their energy indestructible.

Epilogue—Broken Mirrors
(Reflections as the Ceasefire Holds)

Winding

Time
drifts past
soldiers

children
play
in dust

fish
float in
shade

sea
strands
boats

sun
burns
all

like war
so close
you can touch

it winding
your way
home

Solstice

i

Darkness cool and short
relieves the solstice heat
while the earth stealthily slips
around toward winter.

ii

Dogs darken barks
at sight of shadows & eclipses
but dance high, with wild glee,
when they see glinting waves.

iii

Tree bark peels away
only to display colors
beyond gray, brown,
or black imagining.

iv

Peeling my eyes open,
though sticky—closed they'd
give me ways to see this world
unravel from my dreams.

v

Summer opens as its end
starts—long day migrating to
long night—without my noticing
cold harmony under hot melody

vi
as I end my journey into
this land estranged and
strangling, expanding
and contracting around me.

Broken mirrors

i

Born between the Great Lakes and the Big Muddy
I have lived most of my life near large and flowing
waters. Hardwood forests and evergreen patches
clump through these lands where I breathed and
loved to walk alone.

ii

Now dry *Wadis*, a Salt Sea
that supports no life, a few scattered acacia trees
and a rare spring feeding a small water fall drip
onto an almost blank landscape-painting that
wills itself to not quite cohere.

iii

When I visited
here it felt so familiar, like a home or land
where I lived a past life. When I moved
here we became estranged, like old lovers
who shift from infatuated mysterious-others
to over-familiar reflections of ourselves.

iv

Shards
of broken mirror reflect cracked bits of the world
and no painting completes the picture in the
shadowed mind. People I love live here—and there,
too—where I still hide myself in bits of slivered light,
pentimenti revelations beneath the gesso that reveal
and hide the world, which comes toward us in sparks.

Here does not live in me

i

Nameless lizards, rock rabbits, ibex—a desert landscape
sloping down to the Salt Sea, an occasional acacia—
I recognize these, but they don't recognize me.
I lack the proper paperwork for them, crossing from
wet marshes, rivers, lakes into this aged, dry place.
My visa expired while I traveled, like my dreams
of poetry, inspiration, mysticism—torn from my hands
at the border, thrown out. *You think this is your home?*
The desert laughs at me. You don't know how to swim
in the rock and sand; you don't know how to set sail
on our heat waves. I live here—

                              —but here does not live in me.

Layers of war lay buried beneath the wet soil of where
I came from, but these are nothing to the dry layers piled
upon each tel, around every bubbling spring here.
The bitter, embattled, blood-thirsty desert demands
sacrifices, does not easily yield its fruits, edible or poisonous.
How could I imagine that this would be my home?

ii

Night slopes down from the cliffs, shadowed specter
of an ancestor of death, a precursor that still haunts
hillsides. Where I came from, wet caves hid
this dark hunger. Here, the bones of this shade
burn my feet, so I trek barefoot into a trickle
of water, green slicked rocks—the hints
of what once flowed from heart to spirit to mind
before ink scarred paper with it and dried it out.

None of this makes much sense. It never did.
I came here to draw another line in shifting
dust, to demarcate there from here. And yet
neither here nor there are anywhere outside
my somnolent and thoughtless pursuit of place,

a dreamless world looking for its own future
reflected in my disembodiment.

Not yet at home

What feels familiar
Pedaling between two children
who ride the bike with me as we
head over to the train station,
a music class—happy together.

Beneath the surface
Cycling through war, peace,
the anxiety between
two states slicing
through our sanity
in thin strips of calm
clamped tightly between
blasts of light signaling
another migraine.

Screaming at me
Waxing or waning moon
soothes above slow waves,
shallow water, warm air, as
children play in a night sea—
listening for an air-raid siren—
and someone loses his head
across the border—like me,
he is both American and Israeli.

About the Author

Michael Dickel has two previous books of poetry: *The World Behind It, Chaos...* (2009) and *Midwest / Mid-East: March 2012 Poetry Tour* (2012). He was managing editor for arc-23 (2014) and co-editor of Voices Israel 2010 (Vol. 36). His poetry, short fiction, and essays have appeared in print and online journals since 1987. His poetry has been translated into Italian, Romanian, Tamil, and Hebrew. He currently is the Chair of the Israel Association of Writers in English and teaches at HaKibbutzim College of Education, Technology and the Arts in Tel Aviv while living in Jerusalem.

www.ingramcontent.com/pod-product-compliance
Lightning Source LLC
Chambersburg PA
CBHW061512040426
42450CB00008B/1588